# LET'S MAKE AN OPERA!

# LET'S MAKE AN OPERA!

AN ENTERTAINMENT FOR YOUNG PEOPLE
IN THREE ACTS

*including*

# THE LITTLE SWEEP

A CHILDREN'S OPERA

*by*

ERIC CROZIER

*Music by*

BENJAMIN BRITTEN

HAWKES & SON
(LONDON LTD.)

*Sole Selling Agents:*
BOOSEY & HAWKES LTD.

New York . Paris
Buenos Aires . Sydney . Cape Town . Toronto . Bonn

LET'S MAKE AN OPERA! is in three acts. The first two acts are in the form of a play, and illustrate the preparation and rehearsal of "The Little Sweep," a children's opera which is performed in Act Three.

## CHARACTERS

*Of the play.*  *Of the opera.*
GLADYS PARWORTHY . MISS BAGGOTT, the housekeeper.
[*Contralto*]
NORMAN CHAFFINCH . BLACK BOB, the sweepmaster *and*
[*Bass*]  TOM, the coachman.
MAX WESTLETON . . . CLEM, Black Bob's assistant *and*
[*Tenor*]  ALFRED, the gardener.
PAMELA WILTON . . . ROWAN, the nursery-maid.
[*Soprano*]
ANNE DOUGALL . . . JULIET BROOK [aged 14].
[*Soprano*]
MR. HARPER . . . . THE CONDUCTOR of the opera.

## CHILDREN

BRUCE . . . . . . . Gay Brook [aged 16].
MONICA . . . . . . Sophie Brook [aged 10].
PETER . . . . . . John Crome [aged 14].
MAVIS . . . . . . . Tina Crome [aged 8].
RALPH . . . . . . Hugh Crome [aged 8].
JOHN . . . . Sam, the new sweepboy [aged 8].

It is suggested that the names of the actual performers be used for the characters of the play.

# ACT ONE

## SCENE ONE

[*The drawing-room of MRS. PARWORTHY'S house. A piano, two armchairs, standard-lamps and a door in the back wall.*
*When the CURTAIN rises the stage is in darkness. The LIGHTS fade in, to show GLADYS PARWORTHY seated in an armchair by the fire, with all the CHILDREN grouped around her on stools and cushions. ANNE and PAMELA share the other armchair between them: NORMAN CHAFFINCH is on the piano stool, away from the main group.*
*The LIGHT is concentrated on the main group by a standard-lamp, and the feeling is of eager attention to the story GLADYS has promised them. ANNE has a notepad and a pencil.*]

GLADYS
   Are you all comfortable?
ALL
   Yes, thank you! Very comfortable!
GLADYS
   Then I'll begin. The story I am going to tell you took place in Suffolk long before I was born . . .
MAVIS
   Is it a true story?
GLADYS
   True as true! It actually happened to my grandmother.

CHILDREN
: Good!
GLADYS
: Juliet was her name—Juliet Brook—and she lived at Iken Hall, a big Elizabethan house on the banks of the River Alde. It was a lonely house, miles from a village, surrounded by trees where herons nested and owls screamed at night.
RALPH
: It's going to be a ghost story!
CHILDREN
: Is it? Ooooh! I don't like ghosts!
PAMELA
ANNE
: Ssssh!
GLADYS
: When the story begins Juliet was fourteen. She had a brother called Gay . . .
RALPH
: That isn't a boy's name!
GLADYS
: It was *his* name!—and a younger sister, Sophie.
ANNE [*noting*]
: ' Juliet, Gay and Sophie.'
GLADYS
: Their cousins were staying with them for the Christmas holidays . . .
MAVIS
: What were *their* names?
GLADYS
: John, Hughie and Tina. Hughie and Tina were twins.
ANNE [*noting*]
: ' John, Hughie and Tina.'
MONICA
: How old were they?
PAMELA
: Children! we'll never get to the story if you ask so many questions!

NORMAN
  Go on, Gladys!
GLADYS
  Holidays were coming to an end, and it was nearly time for the cousins to go home to Woodbridge, where they lived. They had brought their own nursery-maid to look after them and that was just as well, for all the children loved Rowan, but not one of them liked Miss Baggott.
PAMELA
  Miss Baggott! She doesn't sound very nice!
GLADYS
  She wasn't! A crusty, cantankerous, overbearing old housekeeper with a sharp word always biting her tongue!
NORMAN
  Sorry to interrupt, Gladys, but *when* did this story happen?
ANNE
  I was wondering that!
GLADYS
  Soon after the turn of the century—in eighteen hundred and nine, or ten.
  [*Anne notes the date.*]
NORMAN
  Oh! Jane Austen period!
BRUCE
  George the Fourth!
PAMELA
  Muslin frocks and poke bonnets!
CHILDREN
  Sssh!
GLADYS
  Country houses in those days had big open hearths and winding brick chimneys. When they needed sweeping, little boys were sent up into the soot and the darkness

to scrape them clean. Sam Sparrow was a sweep-boy like that. Only eight years old, poor child!

CHILDREN
Eight!

ANNE
Only eight!

GLADYS
His father was a waggoner, and so dreadfully poor that there was nothing for it but selling little Sam to Black Bob the sweepmaster. Oh, he was a ruffian, Black Bob was! Black inside and out, and his son Clem was as cruel as his wicked father. Just imagine poor Sammy's feelings when they took him to Iken Hall, stripped all the clothes off him and drove him up into the blackness of his first chimney.

GIRLS
Stripped him!

BOYS
Poor Sam!

GLADYS
He climbed and he scraped, and then he climbed a bit higher and scraped again, choking with soot, and up he went, and up—till he found himself wedged in the neck of the flue so that he couldn't move up or down at all. He was frantic, as well he might have been. He shouted "Help! Help! I'm stuck!" Luckily Juliet and the others heard him.

PETER
How did they get him down the chimney?

GLADYS
Black Bob had tied a long rope round his waist in case of accidents. They tugged on that and—Crash!—down he tumbled.

MONICA
They might have killed him!

MAVIS
   Poor little boy!
ANNE
   What a shock for him!
PETER
   I'd like to kick Black Bob!
RALPH
   Clem, too!
GLADYS
   There they were—six young children in nice clean clothes, with a filthy little blackamoor lying in the fireplace and sobbing as though his heart would break. All they could get out of him was "Please don't send me up again!" Over and over again he said it.
NORMAN
   Good moment for music!
MAVIS
   Whatever did they do with him?
GLADYS
   What would you have done with him! Hand him over to the sweeps?
CHILDREN [*indignant*]
   No!
GLADYS
   Would you tell Miss Baggott?
CHILDREN
   No fear!
JOHN
   I know! I'd hide him!
CHILDREN
   Of course! *Hide* him!
GLADYS
   That's exactly what Juliet and the others did. First they laid a trail of sooty footsteps to the window, to deceive the sweeps into thinking Sam had run away . . .

ANNE
> Jolly clever of them!

GLADYS
> ... and then they hid him in the toy-cupboard among their hoops and dolls for a whole day and a night!

BRUCE
> Didn't Miss Baggott find out?

GLADYS
> They were too clever for her! Not only did they bath Sammy and feed him and dress him in clean clothes, but they managed to smuggle him out of the house under her very eyes!

GIRLS [excited]
> Did they?

BOYS
> How? Tell us how?

GLADYS
> It was time for the cousins to go back to Woodbridge. Sam went with them in the top of a trunk. They let him out as soon as they were clear of the house, and off they went down the high-road as merry as crickets, to the rattle and gallop of the horses' feet.

MONICA
> I do hope he lived happy ever after!

GLADYS
> He did! Juliet's uncle took pity on him and set him to work in the gardens at Woodbridge. When my mother was a girl, old Samuel Sparrow had grown to be head-gardener. He used to give her apricots on her birthday.

MAVIS
> How kind of him!

GLADYS
> Well, there's my little story. Do you like it?

ANNE
> I think it's a most lovely story! Thank you ever so much, Mrs. Parworthy!

CHILDREN [*speaking together: enthusiastically*]
   So do I! It's true, too!
   I did enjoy it!
   I'm glad they tricked Miss Baggott!
   Horrid those sweeps were!
   Weren't the children clever!
GLADYS
   Do *you* like it, Norman?
      [*NORMAN gets up and walks around the group in the shadow of the room. The eyes of the others follow him*]
NORMAN
   Of course I do! It's true and it's simple—just the sort of story I *do* like! The question is, will it make an opera?
GLADYS
   You are our composer! You must decide.
NORMAN
   Annie, read out the list of characters.
ANNE [*reading from her notes*]
   First there are two sweeps—Black Bob and Clem . . .
NORMAN
   Bass and light tenor.
ANNE
   Miss Baggott the housekeeper . . .
NORMAN
   Contralto. That's a part for you Gladys!
GLADYS
   I expected that!
ANNE
   Rowan, the nursery-maid from Woodbridge . . .
PAMELA
   Oh, I *must* sing Rowan!
NORMAN
   Soprano, anyway.
ANNE
   There are three girls—Juliet, Sophie and Tina. The boys are Gay, John and Hughie, and Sam makes four.

11

RALPH
: Just right!

BRUCE
: There are four of us!

GLADYS
: It fits beautifully, if Annie plays Juliet.

ANNE
: I'm too old for that!

GLADYS
: Not on the stage, dear! You won't look a day more than fourteen.

PAMELA
: Honestly you won't!

NORMAN
: Clem's a difficulty. We've no tenor.

GLADYS
: We'll find one.

NORMAN
: Apart from him the cast is complete—but can we make the opera?

CHILDREN
: Certainly we can!

NORMAN
: In ten weeks?

CHILDREN
: Yes!

NORMAN
: I wonder . . .!

PAMELA
: Norman, there is just one thing I must say before we go any further . . .

NORMAN
: Come on, then!

GLADYS
: What is it, Pamela?

PAMELA
: I agree with you absolutely about Mrs. Parworthy's story. It has lots of musical possibilities and dramatic ones too, but I can't help wondering if we are right to think of doing it as an opera.

CHILDREN
: Oh, Pam! Don't be a spoil-sport!

GLADYS
: Quiet, children! Let her speak.

PAMELA
: I like opera, but most people don't. They think it's stuffy and old-fashioned and hopelessly artificial, and you can't really blame them when they hardly ever have the chance of seeing really good performances.

ANNIE
: They queue up for Gilbert and Sullivan.

PAMELA
: Yes, but that isn't opera.

NORMAN
: Operetta!

PAMELA
: It would be stupid to work for months and make something no-one wants to see. Won't it be safer to forget about opera and turn the story into a play?

CHILDREN
: Oh, no! Not a play!
We did one last year!
I want to sing!

NORMAN
: Certainly it would be *easier* to do a play . . .

GLADYS
: ' Easier '—but would it be *better*?

CHILDREN
: We want to do an *opera*!

NORMAN

Pamela, I am sure you are right from a practical point of view. People *do* like plays more than opera . . .

ANNE

You can understand a play quicker the first time, because it shows people like us talking about ordinary things . . .

GLADYS

Annie's got it! Most plays talk the language of commonsense. Opera is very like Shakespeare—it speaks in a magic language of its own, and because it isn't tied to everyday words and phrases, it can reveal all the wonderful and terrible and exciting things that lie beneath the surface of everyday life.

ANNE [*suddenly*]

I've just remembered something!

NORMAN

What is it?

ANNE

It's about a Chinese student!

PAMELA

A Chinese student!

GLADYS

Is it another story?

CHILDREN

One of Annie's jokes!

ANNE

Well, you see, this particular Chinese student was taking an examination in English literature and the very first question on his exam. paper asked him to define what poetry was, so he thought for a long, long time and then he wrote down one tiny sentence— [*she giggles*]—"Poetry consists of gists and piths."

GIRLS

Poetry consists of what?

BOYS

Fish and chips?

ANNE [*giggling more*]
All he wrote was "Poetry consists of gists and piths."
PAMELA
What's funny about that?
ANNE
It wasn't meant to be funny! He thought about it for an awful long time and he was deadly serious, and what he wrote was *true!* Music is just the same as he said poetry was. It cuts to the heart of things—it shows you their gists and their piths, [*She giggles again*]. Muthik conthith of giths and piths!
MONICA
Aren't operas always about love?
CHILDREN [*scornfully*]
Love!
ANNE
I don't see why. They can be about anything—anything that lends itself to music.
GLADYS
What about my little sweep? Does he lend himself?
ANNE
Certainly he does!
NORMAN
Plenty of music there!—lashings of it! Look here! I want to try a very simple experiment.
CHILDREN
Experiment? Fine!
[*NORMAN crosses to the piano and switches on the standard-lamp beside it.*]
NORMAN
Johnnie, come over here!
JOHN [*getting up*]
Are you going to experiment on me?
MONICA
Don't hurt him!

NORMAN [*laughing*]
 It's not that sort of experiment!
 [*The CHILDREN get up and collect round the piano.*]
NORMAN
 Pam, you remember that moment in the story when the little sweep is sobbing in the fireplace?
PAMELA
 "Please don't send me up again"?
NORMAN
 That's it. Johnnie, I want you to say that to us.
JOHN
 Say what he said?
NORMAN
 Just speak it. Go on!
CHILDREN
 Go on, Johnnie!
NORMAN
 What are you waiting for?
JOHN
 I feel shy!
CHILDREN
 Silly baby!
NORMAN
 Peter, you come and say it.
JOHN
 No! I'm all right now. Here we go! "Please don't send me up again!"
NORMAN
 Say it once more, as movingly as you can.
JOHN
 "Please don't send me up again!"—Easy!
BRUCE
 Where's the experiment?
NORMAN
 Now sing it. I'll give you the notes. [*He plays the phrase on the piano.*\*] Got it?

\* (Vocal Score No. v)

JOHN
  Once more, please.
NORMAN [*playing the phrase again*]
  Sing it twice. First time rising a semitone on the last note, second time dropping a semitone. [*He plays the phrase that way.*] Off you go!
    [*JOHN sings the phrase twice, with appropriate chords.*]
CHILDREN
  Oh, yes! Much better than speaking!
NORMAN
  Do you see, Pamela? When he speaks he might just as well be saying "Please don't send me out to buy an evening paper!" Mind you, Johnnie, I'm not criticising you!
GLADYS
  No one expects a ten year old to be a trained actor.
NORMAN
  When he sings, you can hear the heartbreak in the musical phrase.
GLADYS
  Have we convinced you, Pamela? Opera?—or play?
CHILDREN
  Opera!
PAMELA
  You needn't have bothered about convincing me! I've been on your side all along, but I thought we should spare a thought for the thousands and thousands of people who only think of opera in terms of outsize sopranos and swans going backwards.
NORMAN
  There's plenty else to amuse them! What we've got to think about is the amount of work it will take. I'll write the music, and proud to do it. Who is going to write the words?
CHILDREN
  Annie! Annie!

ANNE

    Me?—I couldn't—I couldn't do that!

CHILDREN

    Yes, you could!

GLADYS

    You write poetry, dear!

ANNE

    Och, that's only wee scrappity bits of things to amuse myself—nothing like writing an opera! I don't even know how to begin. Does Norman write the music first and I fit words to it afterwards,—or is it the other way round?

NORMAN

    We work together, Annie, all along. What's an opera for?—to tell a story through words and music. Gladys has given us the story. We have a family of characters,—sweeps, children, housekeeper and nursery-maid. We know pretty well what happens to them—now we must decide *how* it will happen. We want them to sing, but it would be terribly dull if they only sang by turns or if they all sang all the time. So we must aim to blend our characters in as many different combinations as we can—duets, trios, alone sometimes, or all together, just like a painter who mixes blue, red and yellow to make the colours he needs.

ANNE

    Is that how it's done!

NORMAN

    After working for a week or two on the story, the characters will begin to come alive. Then you will find the words lining up on the end of your pen, and I'll be hearing the notes they call for.

ANNE

    It sounds wonderful when you put it like that, Norman. Are you sure you're not exaggerating?

NORMAN
    Of course I am!
GLADYS
    He's leaving out the hard work. We all know you're not afraid of that!
PAMELA
    You agree, don't you, Annie!
GLADYS
    Go on, Annie, say you'll do it!
CHILDREN    [overlapping]
    Say Yes, Annie! Please say Yes!
NORMAN
    Come on, Annie, you can't escape!
ANNE [hesitant]
    Well—how long have we got?
NORMAN
    That's another question! I want to know that, too!
GLADYS
    I think we should aim to give the performance in the last week of the school holidays . . .
CHILDREN
    Good! After Christmas! [or whenever it is.]
GLADYS
    That allows us ten weeks for everything. Writing the music . . .
NORMAN
    Copying it . . .
ANNE
    Writing the words . . .
PAMELA
    Typing them . . .
GIRLS
    Learning the music . . .
BOYS
    Learning the words . . .
NORMAN
    Building scenery . . .

PAMELA
>    Making properties . . .
GLADYS
>    Sewing dresses . . .
ANNE
>    Finding an orchestra . . .
NORMAN
>    Hiring a hall . . .
PAMELA
>    Printing tickets . . .
GLADYS
>    Rehearsing . . .
GIRLS
>    Rehearsing . . .
BOYS
>    Rehearsing . . .
ALL
>    And *rehearsing!*
ANNE
>    It's impossible!
NORMAN
>    Stark, staring, impossible!
GLADYS
>    But we'll do it—somehow we'll do it!
CHILDREN
>    We'll *do* it!
PAMELA
>    I hate to think what will happen to your homework.
GIRLS
>    Bother homework!
BOYS
>    This is much more important!
GLADYS
>    Rehearsals for Scene One will begin a month from now . . .
ANNE
>    A month!

NORMAN
   Crazy!
GLADYS
   Three evenings a week and each week-end. You can rehearse here to begin with. Everyone but Norman and Anne must help with scenery and costumes. By the way, what *about* scenery?
PAMELA
   We've some bits left over from *The Pirates of Penzance*.
ANNE
   Norman and I can plan the opera in one set.
NORMAN
   The children's nursery!
ANNE
   Two doors, a fireplace and a window . . .
BRUCE
   And the toy-cupboard!
ANNE
   *And* the toy-cupboard. We could start bang off with the arrival of the sweeps dragging Sam into the room, which is all muffled up with dust-sheets . . .
NORMAN
   Good idea! Miss Baggott bullies them along . . .
ANNE
   And Rowan's overcome with pity for the poor little white boy, who stands shivering with terror . . .
NORMAN
   They shove him up the chimney and leave him there . . .
ANNE
   Till the children creep into the nursery . . .
PETER
   Why?
MONICA
   They're playing Hide and Seek!
CHILDREN
   Hide and Seek! Of course!

ANNE
> . . . and they hear Sammy calling out "Help! Help! I'm stuck! I'm suffocating! Pull me down!"

GLADYS [*interrupting them*]
> Annie and Norman, you can go on planning till the cows come home, but it's high time I sent these children off to bed.

CHILDREN
> Do let us stay! Five minutes more!

GLADYS
> No more tonight. Run home and tell your fathers and mothers they'll soon be hearing you at Covent Garden!

MONICA
> Coo! won't the girls at school be jealous!

MAVIS
> Green! They'll be *green!*

GLADYS
> The children are off, Norman!

NORMAN
> Hi! Wait! This is a great occasion! You can't slink away like that!

ANNE
> We ought to celebrate!

PAMELA
> A stirrup-cup or something!

GLADYS
> I know! A musical toast!

CHILDREN
> Oh yes! A musical toast!

NORMAN
> A musical toast! Here you are! 'Let's make an opera!'—sung in thirds—fortississississimo! [*He plays a heroic phrase on the piano, repeats it singing himself, then stands and conducts the others.*]

ALL [*singing*]

# TOAST

*to black-out. After applause the piano begins playing "Sweep! Sweep!"\* and the lights fade in again on NORMAN, who is sitting at the piano playing and singing the song.*
*The time is a month later. It is evening and only the piano-lamp is lit. Downstage R. a scale model of the opera set stands on a table with a lamp to illuminate it, but this is not yet lit. ANNE opens the door and comes in.]*

## SCENE TWO

ANNE
   Good evening, Norman!
NORMAN
   Hallo, Annie! Where have you sprung from?
ANNE
   I was waiting outside till you finished.
NORMAN
   Eavesdropping!
ANNE
   Och, you don't mind, do you! I had a good listen to the Sweep's Song you were playing.
NORMAN
   Did you now!
ANNE
   Excuse me for saying so, Norman, but isn't it a wee bit on the long side for the sweeps?
NORMAN
   I've had an idea about that. Guess what?
ANNE
   You tell me—I'm a rotten guesser.
NORMAN
   The whole audience is going to sing it!

\* (Vocal Score No. 1)

ANNE
>   The audience sing the sweep's song!

NORMAN
>   Yes! we haven't got a chorus like most operas, so we'll make them work instead.

ANNE
>   Norman, they'll never do it!

NORMAN
>   Yes, they will. They'll sing it as an Overture. Come here while I show you.

ANNE [*crossing to the piano*]
>   I can't see my Auntie Mary singing. She sounds bad enough in church!

NORMAN
>   The tune is easy. Sing the first verse with me.
>   [*NORMAN plays, and they sing the first verse together.*]

ANNE ⎫
NORMAN ⎬ [*singing*]
>   Sweep! Sweep!
>   Saddle your donkey and set on your way!
>   There's chimneys need sweeping at Iken today.
>   Bring brushes and scrapers and baskets and sacks
>   To harvest the soot from our chim-in-ey stacks.

ANNE
>   It's a marvellous idea if it doesn't fall flat.

NORMAN
>   That's up to the audience! Now, what I want from you is two more songs for them to sing in the intervals.

ANNE
>   Two more! For pity's sake!

NORMAN
>   One at the end of Scene One—*Sammy's Bath*. We can't show them that, so they must sing about it instead.

ANNE [*making a note*]
>   End of Scene One—*Sammy's Bath*.

NORMAN
 And a Night Song after Scene Two.
ANNE [*writing*]
 ' Night Song '—when Sam is hidden in the cupboard. How many verses?
NORMAN
 Four. Triplets, if you can.
ANNE
 Any special metre?
NORMAN
 No—but I want it to be quiet and serene.
ANNE
 You know what, Norman! A Night Song would give us the chance of making the audience sing in parts—always supposing they sing anyway!
NORMAN
 That's a fine idea!
ANNE
 A sort of musical game about the things you might hear in the country at night! The ripple of the river, a sheep coughing . . .
NORMAN
 Barking dogs . . .
ANNE
 The chime of a distant church bell, birds . . .
NORMAN
 Birds!—*Birds!* Owls and herons!
ANNE
 A competition of birds! Let me try something on those lines, with different cries for different birds!
NORMAN
 Tu-whit-tu-whoo!
ANNE
 Kaaah! Kaaah!
NORMAN
 What's that? A bullfrog?

ANNE
   It's a heron, silly! Are you in a hurry for this?
NORMAN
   Everything's a hurry! My hair is grey with hurry! I shan't draw a good deep breath till the opera is finished, and then our troubles will just be beginning. Have you brought me some more of Scene Two?
ANNE
   It's finished.
NORMAN
   Well done!
ANNE
   I got up early this morning to write the big ensemble after Juliet faints. Here it is—two verses for Miss Baggott, two for Rowan and one verse that the children sing in chorus. Will that be enough?
NORMAN
   Let me see it.
         [*ANNE gives him two sheets of paper*].
ANNE
   It begins right after the faint.
NORMAN [*beginning to read*]
   Um—hum!
ANNE
   I've tried to make the words simple and clear for singing. You know, Norman, writing a libretto has taught me an awful lot. When I began, I thought any words would do, but now I've learnt to write with my ears open and to choose words that have a fine bright ring to them, like silver coins. It's a fascinating job picking out the words that sing from those that only mumble. I'm ever so grateful to you for asking me to work on it.
NORMAN
   Well, if we get through this opera alive, we must write some more.

ANNE

~~Oh, yes, please!~~ ~~How are those~~ verses for the ~~ensemble?~~

NORMAN

I may need one verse more for the children, but I will tell you that later. Can I keep this?

ANNE

Certainly! I have a copy.

[*PAMELA knocks at the door and comes in quickly.*]

PAMELA

Norman, I'm late! Are you cross with me? Hallo, Annie!

ANNE

Hallo, Pamela!

NORMAN

Good evening, Pamela! Where have you been?

PAMELA

I went round to Miss Watson's after tea for the vocal parts, and she kept me waiting for the last page.

NORMAN

Is that the Scene One ensemble?

PAMELA [*giving him some sheets of music*]

Yes—"Is he wounded?" for all the children.

NORMAN

I want to begin rehearsing that this evening. What is the time now?

PAMELA

Ten to six.

ANNE

They are coming at six.

NORMAN

Just time to run through your aria, Pamela.

PAMELA

Oh, thank you!

ANNE

You don't mind if I stay and listen?

PAMELA }
NORMAN }
   No, of course not!
NORMAN
   Put the other light on.
      [*ANNE switches on the standard-lamp and sits in the armchair.*]
PAMELA
   Shall I try it without the music?
NORMAN
   Much better if you can. Oh, Annie! I've had to change the order of your verses in this song.
ANNE
   How's that?
NORMAN
   The sweeps rush off looking for Sam. Great excitement and hurry—like this. [*He plays some of the Sweep's trio.*\*] You gave Rowan a quiet verse immediately after that, but I want to keep up the excitement and show how upset she is by the rage of the sweeps. You don't mind.
ANNE
   Of course I don't.
NORMAN
   Pamela, I want you to listen first of all to these spread chords that begin your song. Each one of them is a cry of sympathy for the little sweep-boy. [*He plays them.*]† Think of the sweeps chasing him along the river-wall like a hound after a fox, and let us hear desperate pity for him in your phrases. Try it!
      [*NORMAN plays and PAMELA sings.*]
PAMELA [*singing*]
   Run, poor sweepboy! Run much faster!
   Leave the road and seek the hedge.
   Close behind you comes your master,
   Jealous of his privilege!

\* (Vocal Score No. vii)     † (Vocal Score No. viii)

NORMAN

Now a long pause and a change of key. Next verse more restrained, but deeply sympathetic still.

PAMELA [*singing*]

    *Far along the frozen river*
    *Where the highway skirts the sedge,*
    *Distant echoes make Sam shiver*
    *As he leaves the water's edge.*

NORMAN

Third section. You urge him to escape as fast as he can.

PAMELA [*singing*]

    *Run, poor boy! Oh, do not slacken!*
    *Black Bob follows swift behind.*
    *Cruel men will soil and blacken*
    *Childish heart and childish mind!*

NORMAN

The passion dies down, and you feel a great longing to help the little boy.

PAMELA [*singing*]

    *How I wish that I could aid you!*
    *I would help you to evade*
    *Those who hate you and degrade you*
    *In their filthy sweeping trade!*

NORMAN

And as the emotion surges up in you again, the children creep very gently out of their hiding-place and surprise you.

PAMELA

Does it sound any better, Norman?

NORMAN

Much better—so long as you remember that the song is in four clear sections, each one with a mood and a colour of its own.

PAMELA

I will!

ANNE

The words are beautifully clear!

NORMAN
   There speaks a librettist!
ANNE
   Oh, Norman!—I didn't mean that—but they *are!*
   [*The door opens and* GLADYS *enters followed by all the children except* MAVIS *and* RALPH. *They wear coats and scarves and are laden with odd-shaped parcels.*]
GLADYS [*in gay good spirits*]
   Here we are! Battered but unbowed! What a day! I would never have reached home alive without these children!
NORMAN
   What an entrance! We ought to have something like that in our opera!
GLADYS
   Oh, my poor feet! Torture!
CHILDREN
   Where shall we put the parcels?
GLADYS
   Anywhere you like! The house looks more like a museum every day.
ANNE
   Take your coats off, children.
GLADYS
   We've been round every junk-shop in town, buying baskets, brushes, buckets, brooms, carpet-beaters and triumph of triumphs!—a hip-bath! A real old-fashioned hip-bath!
PAMELA
   You didn't bring that with you!
CHILDREN
   Yes, we did!
GLADYS
   Ralph and Mavis are carrying it, unless they've fallen by the wayside.

CHILDREN

    No, here they come!

        [*There is a heavy thump on the door. They open it, and RALPH and MAVIS enter, carrying the hip-bath on their heads like a large hat. [If possible they could crawl in beneath it like a clockwork tortoise*].]

ALL

    Hooray! Well done! Bravo!

MAVIS  
RALPH  } [*from underneath*]

    Let us out! Lift it off!

        [*The others help them free.*]

ANNE

    Oh, that's a beauty! Where did you find it?

GLADYS

    I got it for nothing. Mr. Ledbetter said he had fallen over it regularly every morning for the last twenty-six years. He had even complained to the Corporation because the dustman wouldn't take it away.

PAMELA

    Just what we need!

ANNE

    Well done, Mrs. Parworthy!

NORMAN

    I don't know what we should do without you, Gladys!

CHILDREN

    What about us?

RALPH  
MAVIS  }

    What about *us*? We carried the hip-bath!

NORMAN

    Children, I shall express my admiration for each one of you with a small token of my esteem . . .

PETER

    I should jolly well think so!

CHILDREN
 Well, what is it?
NORMAN
 One copy per person of my latest composition—"Is he wounded! Please forgive us!" Words by Miss Dougall.
CHILDREN [disgusted]
 Oooh!
BRUCE
 I thought he meant it!
RALPH
 He's kidding us!
JOHN
 More work!
GLADYS
 Come on, children, time for rehearsal!
MONICA [discovering the scene-model]
 I say, look at this!
MAVIS
 Look, look! A model!
CHILDREN
 Model scenery! Look! Let us see it!
GLADYS
 Oh, yes! I'd forgotten that! Switch on the lamp, Mavis.
ANNE
 I'll put this one out. [She switches off the standard-lamp.]
NORMAN
 This, too. [He switches off the piano light.]
  [Everyone gathers round the scene-model, and the stage is lit only from the glow of it on their faces.]
CHILDREN
 Isn't it lovely?
ANNE
 So pretty and gay!
PAMELA
 Look at the striped wallpaper!

MONICA
    Is it for our opera?
GLADYS
    It is! A real scale-model of the nursery, with two doors . . .
MAVIS
    Fireplace . . .
JOHN
    Window . . .
BRUCE
    Toy cupboard! . . .
GIRLS
    And tiny furniture!
BOYS
    Who made it?
GALDYS
    Max Westleton.
GIRLS
    Who?
GLADYS
    Max Westleton, from the building-office by the station. Oh, and Norman! I've persuaded him to come for an audition this evening!
NORMAN
    You have? Good!
PAMELA
    Is that for the part of Clem?
GLADYS
    That's right. He'll be very nervous, I expect, so will you all be specially nice to him?
CHILDREN
    We will!
NORMAN
    What time is he coming?
GLADYS
    At half-past six.

NORMAN

Heavens! We must get on with the rehearsal. Work, children!

[*The LIGHTS are switched on.*]

Scene One ensemble.

RALPH

Scene One *what?*

NORMAN

Scene One *ensemble*—French for ' together.'

ANNE

*Ensemble*—when we all sing together.

RALPH

Then why not say so?

BRUCE

I thought singing together was called a ' chorus.'

NORMAN

So it is, Bruce. But in this number, each one of you has his own line to sing. You have separate parts, and it's easier to call that an ' ensemble.'

MONICA

It sounds jolly difficult.

NORMAN

Let's try it and see.

GLADYS

Norman, Pam and I aren't in this. We'll be downstairs till you want us.

NORMAN

Right you are! Everyone else round the piano with copies.

[*GLADYS and PAMELA go out. The CHILDREN gather round NORMAN at the piano.*]

This song begins immediately Sammy falls down the chimney. Go from just before that—the last two bars of the shanty. This is your note.

[*NORMAN gives them the note and they sing.*]\*

\* (Vocal Score No. iv.)

CHILDREN [*singing*]
"ONE—TWO—THREE—*JERK!.*"
[*JOHN falls to the floor with a screech.*]
JOHN
"*Owwww . . . wwww!*"
CHILDREN
"*Ooooh! You've killed him!*"
NORMAN
And straightaway the ensemble begins—quick and upset.
ANNE
Before you play the music, Norman, let's read the words through to make sure there are no mistakes.
NORMAN
Take it verse by verse.
ANNE
Monica, you begin!
MONICA [*reading*] "Is he wounded?
ANNE Please forgive us!
PETER Are you very much in pain?
RALPH AND MAVIS All we wanted was to help you!
[AND BRUCE] All we wanted was to help you!
JOHN *Please* don't send me up again!"
RALPH
Sounds daft like that!
PETER
Doesn't mean a thing.
ANNE
It's not meant to be spoken. It's meant to be sung.
NORMAN
Listen to the music now. I'll play you the first verse. What I have done is to join all those little bits of phrases into one long line of melody. There is one strong bar before the melody begins.
[*NORMAN plays the first verse through\*.*]

\* (Vocal Score No. v.)

ANNE

    Fine! You have caught just the right urgency and excitement!

PETER

    It's jolly fast!

CHILDREN

    Too fast!

NORMAN

    Of course it's fast! When someone has an accident you don't look at them and say [he speaks very slowly] "Is——he——wounded?"

                              [RALPH laughs loudly.]

You say [he speaks quickly] "Is he wounded?" I have tried to make this song give that feeling all through.

MONICA

    Can we learn the music, Mr. Chaffinch?

CHILDREN

    Let's learn it!

NORMAN

    Very well—slow tempo till you've got hold of the notes. I'll play just the melody. Off we go!

        [NORMAN plays the melody of the first verse again, in slow time, and the CHILDREN sing their lines rather uncertainly.]

MAVIS

    Please can we have it again?

NORMAN

    One bar . . .

                          [They repeat it, a little better.]

NORMAN

    That's coming. We'll try it a bit quicker, with the accompaniment.

BOYS

    Good!

                [They do the first verse reasonably well.]

NORMAN
> Jolly good for a first go. Now the second verse . . .
> [*The door opens and GLADYS enters.*]

GLADYS
> Terribly sorry to disturb you all, but Max Westleton is here, Norman.

NORMAN
> Oh, is he? Then we must put him out of his misery.

GLADYS
> Waiting for an audition is worse than waiting at the dentist's! Shall I bring him up?

NORMAN
> Yes, please, Gladys.

GLADYS
> Remember, children—treat him gently!

CHILDREN
> We will!
> [*GLADYS goes out.*]

ANNE
> Poor man! it's terrible for him to arrive and find a roomful of people waiting to hear him. I reckon we'd better go out.

CHILDREN
> Oh no! let us stay!

ANNE
> What do you think, Norman?

NORMAN
> He'll have to face a whole hallfull of people if he sings Clem, so he may as well get used to it.

PETER
> Do we shake him by the hand?

ANNE
> Just be yourselves. Be natural!

JOHN

Here they are!
[*The door opens and the CHILDREN quickly line up at either side of it as though forming a guard of honour. GLADYS and PAMELA enter with MAX.*]

GLADYS

Do come in, Mr. Westleton! The children have been rehearsing their new song. This is Ralph—John—Monica—Bruce—Peter—and Annie Dougall, who wrote the words.
[*As each name is mentioned, they shake hands with MAX extra-politely, and say ' How do you do?'*]
You've met Norman Chaffinch already.

MAX

How do you do?

NORMAN

Good evening, Max! Nice of you to come! Sorry to put you through the ordeal of an audition.

MAX

I'm afraid I'm here under false pretences. I wouldn't have dreamt of coming only Mrs. Parworthy was so insistent.

NORMAN

Oh, we all know what Gladys is when she is determined!

GLADYS

Really, Norman! you make me sound like a commercial traveller!

MAX

It's years since I did any singing.

GALDYS

I remember you so well as a soprano in the choir!

MAX

But my voice has broken since then!

NORMAN
   So has mine. I still inflict it on everyone!
CHILDREN [*bringing a chair*]
   Won't you sit down, Mr. Westleton?
MAX
   No, thank you. I'd rather stand.
NORMAN
   Gladys has told you about our little opera. We've begun rehearsals, but we are one man short.
MAX
   When will the performance be?
GLADYS
   Tenth of January . . .
ANNE
   At the Jubilee Hall.
MAX
   Jubilee Hall! In public . . . ?
PAMELA
   Yes, of course.
MAX [*to Gladys*]
   You didn't tell me that! [*to Norman*]. I had no idea it was to be public. I thought you were getting it up to amuse yourselves. I couldn't sing in public!
GIRLS
   Why not?
BOYS
   We're going to!
MAX
   Sing with two or three hundred people watching and listening? I couldn't! You must look for someone else.
GLADYS
   Oh, Mr. Westleton, and you promised.
MAX
   I promised to give an audition—not to sing at the Jubilee Hall! Look at me! I'm a simple middle-class fellow, not an opera-singer.

NORMAN
> Look at us, for that matter! Simple people everyone of us, and we're making this opera for people just like ourselves.

GLADYS
> Look at these children! They're simple enough, but they are going to sing.

CHILDREN
> Yes, look at *us*.

ANNE
> Do sing for us, Mr. Westleton!

PAMELA
> Please sing! We'd love to have you.

MAX
> I hate to disappoint you by refusing . . .

NORMAN
> Of course you do! Sing for us first, and we will talk about the performance afterwards. Did you bring anything with you?

MAX
> I found this Album of English Songs. What about "Early One Morning"?

NORMAN
> Anything you like!

CHILDREN
> Oh, good, he's going to do it!

GLADYS
> Clear a space, children.

PAMELA
> Give him room!
> [*The CHILDREN form a semicircle down stage to listen to MAX, who stands below the door.*]

NORMAN
> Is this the right key for you?

MAX
> I don't know.

NORMAN
> Try it. [*He plays the opening chords*].

MAX
> Too high! I can't get up there.

GLADYS
> Transpose it down, Norman

NORMAN
> How is this? [*He plays the opening in a lower key*].

MAX
> That's comfortable, thank you!

GLADYS
> Now don't be nervous, Mr. Westleton. We are all friends here. We know just how you are feeling.

MAX
> I hope you don't!
> [*NORMAN plays the introduction and MAX sings "Early One Morning." At the end, they all applaud and congratulate him.*]

ALL
> Splendid! Well done! That's fine! You must sing Clem! Good old Max! Just what we want! Hooray!

NORMAN
> Excellent! You can't argue any more with a voice like that! You're just what we have been looking for,
> [*MAX has a sudden panic and bolts for the door. The others follow and bring him back, laughing and all talking at once.*]

ALL
> Oh no, you don't! Come back! He's trying to escape! Don't let him go! Bring him back! He's our Clem! No running away!
> [*The LIGHTS fade out as they pull MAX back into the room, and the CURTAIN falls.*]

THE END OF ACT ONE

# ACT TWO

[*The stage of the hall or theatre just before the dress-rehearsal of "The Little Sweep." The set is already up, but one flat lies on the stage face downward.*
*There is a sound of loud hammering before the CURTAIN rises. When the CURTAIN goes up, NORMAN CHAFFINCH is seen on the stage, hammering a cleat on to the back of the flat. He looks up and sees the audience.*]

NORMAN
  Hi! HI!—Who pulled that curtain?
PETER [*off*]
  I did, Mr. Chaffinch!
NORMAN
  Shut it again, you blithering idiot! Shut it! The hall's full of people!
PETER [*appearing from the prompt corner*]
  I know it is.
NORMAN
  Then what on earth do you want to open the curtain for?
PETER
  Mr. Harper told me to.
NORMAN
  Mr. Harper told you to! Why, in heaven's name? Why?
PETER
  He wants to rehearse with the orchestra.

NORMAN
What! with the curtain up?
PETER
That's what he said.
NORMAN
I don't like it! It gives the whole game away to the audience. Spoils the illusion. It's—it's unprofessional!
PETER
Shall I shut it again?
NORMAN
You'd better leave it now. The damage is done, anyway.

[*Suddenly all the LIGHTS go out.*]

NORMAN
What's happened to the lights? *Lights!*
PETER
That's Bruce fiddling with the switchboard. *Lights*, Bruce!
BRUCE [*off*]
Hold on a minute. I'm changing a fuse.
NORMAN
What a moment to start changing fuses! You're delaying the whole dress-rehearsal! We won't be ready for a week if you play about with fuses!
BRUCE [*off*]
Shan't be a jiffy!
PETER
Do you want help, Bruce?
BRUCE [*off*]
No, thanks!
MAX [*off, calling out*]
Norman, Norman Chaffinch! Where are you?
PETER
There's Max!
NORMAN
Hallo, Max! I'm on stage! Did you get the trunk?

MAX [*off*]
   Yes! I've got it here, but I can't find the door.
PETER
   Stand still, Max! I'll come and help you.
NORMAN
   Bruce! For pity's sake put that fuse back where you got it from and give us some light!
BRUCE [*off*]
   Coming in now!
      [*The RED FOOTLIGHTS slowly fade in.*]
BRUCE [*off*]
   How's that?
NORMAN
   No good at all! Take out the Bengal Fire effect and give us a working light!
PETER
   *Working* light, Bruce!
NORMAN
   A plain, honest-to-goodness bit of ordinary white light!
      [*As he says ' light,' all the LIGHTS come on.*]
   Thank Heavens for that. Now come on stage and leave those fuses alone!
      [*PETER helps MAX through the door with a leather trunk. MAX wears his overcoat.*]
MAX
   Here we are, Norman! Sorry I've been so long, but it took rather a time to find a trunk of the right size.
NORMAN
   At least that one goes through the door.
MAX
   I hope it's big enough for Johnnie.
NORMAN
   It should be. We'll try him in it.

MAX [*calling off*]
>Bruce, bring a duster with you! This trunk is filthy! [*to Norman*] Has Ralph turned up yet?

PETER
>No, he hasn't.

MAX
>Not come *yet?*

NORMAN
>I told him the dress-rehearsal was to begin at half-past seven, bother him! It's always Ralph who is late! Always Ralph!

MAX
>There's no holding him since he got that racing bike with corkscrew handlebars.
>[*BRUCE appears with a dirty piece of rag. NORMAN finishes his hammering.*]
>Oh, Bruce, give this a bit of a rub. It's black with dust and cobwebs.

BRUCE
>O.K., Max! [*He sets to work to clean the trunk*].

MAX
>What are you doing with that flat, Norman?

NORMAN
>I've been moving the cleat down a few inches. It made a rotten join with the fireplace flat—you could see right between them.

MAX
>Poplar's no good for making scenery! It warps all over the place.

NORMAN
>Poplar's not worth the planing. Pine's the stuff—when you can get it. Give me a hand to throw this flat up.

PETER
>Right you are!

NORMAN
> Take the top corners. I'll foot it.
> [*MAX and PETER stoop to lift the top of the flat.*]
> Up to me!
> [*They run it up to the vertical*].
> Steady! Keep your hands well up and lift it back. Lean it against that corner.
> [*They lift the flat and lean it up against another.*]
> Well, we're getting on! Nearly ready!

PETER
> Shall I tell the conductor?

NORMAN
> Oh no! There's plenty to do before he comes? Call everyone on stage for the trunk scene.

PETER
> Righto! I'll call them!
> [*PETER goes off and is heard calling in a loud voice "Everyone on stage, please! Everyone on for the trunk scene!" Other voices take up the call further off.*]

NORMAN
> What's the time now, Max?

MAX
> A quarter to eight.

NORMAN
> It could be worse. I never knew a dress-rehearsal begin on time yet. We shan't be long.

MAX
> I'm going down to make-up.

NORMAN
> Oh no! you don't! We need you for the trunk scene and for putting Sam up the chimney, and Jack Harper has some bits of music to rehearse.

MAX [*looking at the audience*]
> Rather public, isn't it!

NORMAN
 What can we do? It's our own silly fault for beginning late.—Here are the others!
  [*GLADYS comes on stage, followed by everyone else except RALPH. They are all dressed and partially made-up*].
GLADYS
 Norman, the orchestra is getting terribly restless under the stage. It's like a Turkish bath down there.
NORMAN
 Shan't keep them five minutes.
ANNE
 Has anyone seen Ralph?
PAMELA
 He hasn't come yet!
MAVIS
 Isn't he a terror!
JOHN [*seeing the trunk*]
 Is that my trunk?
MONICA
 Coo! not much room for a boy in that!
ANNE
 He'll stifle!
MAX
 No, he won't. I'll punch some air-holes in the back.
NORMAN
 Get in, Johnnie! You'll be best kneeling.
  [*JOHN climbs into the trunk*].
GLADYS
 Poor boy! What a performance!
PETER
 He looks like a sardine in a tin!
NORMAN
 Now shut the lid. How's that?
JOHN [*from inside the trunk*]
 Hurts my neck!

48

MAX
>Open up!—Curl on your side, Johnnie.

ANNE
>Have one of these cushions for your head! There!

NORMAN
>How is it sideways?

JOHN [*trying it*]
>Much better!

NORMAN
>Are you quite comfortable?

JOHN
>Fine, thank you! I'll have a little sleep!

NORMAN
>Stay there for now. We are going to rehearse carrying you out. Is Robert in the pit?

ROBERT [ *from the orchestral pit*]
>Yes! I'm here!

NORMAN
>Trunk scene, Robert! Quickly as you can. Positions, everybody!

PAMELA
>Where shall we go from? Beginning of the recitative?

NORMAN
>Pick it up in the middle. I'll begin with—"*Can't be done, Missus!*"

MAX
>"*Much too heavy!*"

NORMAN
>That's it! And do remember, all of you, that these bits of recitative aren't like full-blown singing. They are a kind of musical conversation. Make them natural!

EVERYONE
>All right. We'll remember!

ROBERT [*from the pit*]
>The bar you come in, Norman. Here's your chord!
>>[*The PIANO plays and they sing.\**]

### Recitative

| | |
|---|---|
| TOM | "Can't be done, Missus! |
| ALFRED | Much too heavy! |
| MISS BAGGOTT | Nonsense! I packed it myself! |
| TOM | Then you'll have to unpack it! |
| MISS BAGGOTT | I'll do nothing of the sort! |
| TOM and ALFRED | Then here she stays! |
| MISS BAGGOTT | The impertinence! |
| TOM | Either that there box is unpacked |
| TOM and ALFRED | Or we leave her where she lies! |
| CHILDREN | Oh, no! |
| TOM and ALFRED | Oh, yes! |
| ROWAN | Mr Tom, we'll help you lift the box! |
| CHILDREN | Yes, please let us help! |
| TOM | Well, that's a fair offer, Miss, and kindly meant! What's your view, Alfred? |
| ALFRED | Very kind indeed! |
| ROWAN | Good! Everyone help lift! |
| CHILDREN | Everyone help lift! |

### Ensemble

ALL
>One and two and—that's the way!
>Up she comes! Hip—hip—hooray!
>Many hands make labour light,
>Now you'll manage her all right!
>>[*As they sing, they carry the trunk to the door and go out with it.*]

\* (Vocal Score No. XVII)

NORMAN [*coming back on stage*]
 Right! Come back everyone! Don't bother about the trunk!
VOICES
 Back again! On stage! Leave the trunk! Out you come, Johnnie!
  [*They all come back, and JOHN with them.*]
GLADYS
 That works well.
NORMAN
 I'm glad John is a featherweight!
ANNE
 Do you want to do it again, Norman?
NORMAN
 There's no time!
MAX
 What about you, Johnnie?
JOHN
 It's easy for me! All I have to do is lie down.
GLADYS
 You know, I'm awfully worried about Ralph. Someone had better put a coat on and go round to his house. This is getting serious!
ANNE
 He can't have forgotten the day?
NORMAN
 Of course he can't. I spoke to him just before tea!
PAMELA
 He might have had an accident . . .
GLADYS
 That new bike! He dashes about on it like a dirt-track rider.
MAX
 Norman, I'll go round. It won't take more than ten minutes.

GLADYS
>   Really, its too bad of him!
>   [RALPH *appears behind them.*]

PAMELA [*seeing him*]
>   Talk of angels!

CHILDREN
>   Look . . . !

GLADYS [*expressively*]
>   Angels—!
>   [RALPH *saunters on to the stage, wearing a long overcoat, and with a bicycle-pump sticking out under one arm. He is eating cake from a paper bag, and saunters down stage to the indignant group.*]

GLADYS
>   Ralph! Where have you been? Why are you so late, you terrible boy!

NORMAN
>   Half past seven, I told you! Half past seven, dressed and made up! Look at the time now! Eight o'clock!

GLADYS
>   You've kept the entire dress-rehearsal waiting! Look at all those people out there! You've kept *them* waiting!

NORMAN
>   Hundreds and hundreds of them—nice, good-mannered, respectable people—kept waiting through the carelessness of one insignificant schoolboy!

GLADYS
>   Well, say something! Tell them you are sorry!

PAMELA
>   He can't even say, ' Sorry.'

CHILDREN
>   Ralph, say ' Sorry!'
>   [RALPH *looks quite unmoved by this tirade, but he swallows and mumbles out ' Sorry' to the*

*audience before putting some more cake in his mouth.*]

ANNE
Where's his costume, anyway?

PAMELA
Ralph, where's your costume?

GLADYS
You promised faithfully to bring it with you!

NORMAN
Don't say he's forgotten his costume!

CHILDREN
Oh Ralph! You silly donkey! He's forgotten it! How could he? No costume!

GLADYS
I give up, Norman! There's nothing to be done with a boy like that!

NORMAN
Oh, yes, there is! He can run all the way home again and fetch it! Of all the silly crackbrained ideas . . .! Fancy coming to a dress-rehearsal without your costume! Idiot!

[*RALPH puts a large bit of cake in his mouth, slowly unbuttons his coat, opens it and shows himself fully dressed for the stage beneath.*]

EVERYONE
Oh! you rascal! Stupid! Thinks he's funny! Throw him out! That's a rotten joke! Pulling our legs! Oh, Ralph!

RALPH [*well-pleased*]
Ha! Ha! Ha! Caught you all!

[*The CONDUCTOR comes into the pit and calls up to the stage.*]

CONDUCTOR
I say, Norman!—*Norman!*

ANNE
It's Mr. Harper!

NORMAN

Hallo? Yes?

CONDUCTOR

Do you know what time it is? Nearly eight o'clock!

NORMAN

We're almost ready! I just want to rehearse Sam up the chimney and down again.

CONDUCTOR

How long will that take? Five minutes?

NORMAN

Not so much! Three minutes at most. Why don't you rehearse one of the audience songs while you wait?

CONDUCTOR

I'd like to do that. I'll start them on Number One.

NORMAN

Good. We'll give you the house lights. Bruce, put them up, please!

BRUCE

Yes, Mr. Chaffinch! [*He goes off stage to do so.*]

CONDUCTOR

Anyone who isn't busy on stage, please help me with "*Sweep! Sweep!*"

CHILDREN

Yes! We will!

[*The Conductor turns to the audience and rehearses them in the first audience song—first with piano and then with orchestra.\**]

*At the same time the stage is busy rehearsing SAM'S going up the chimney. First he is pushed up by the two SWEEPS and lifted out at the back. Next, the CHILDREN run through the movements of pulling him down, and at the climax he is dropped into the fireplace from above. Each of these actions can be rehearsed once or twice, as required.*

\* (Vocal Score No. 1.)

*When the stage-rehearsal is done, the CHILDREN drift down stage and join in the audience song, while MAX, NORMAN and PETER, run the flat into position, cleat it up and arrange the set for the opening of the opera. Any other stage business can be put in here that will keep the scene alive while the audience rehearsal continues.] At the end of the audience song:*

CONDUCTOR
Norman! they know the first song well!
GLADYS
It sounds fine!
ANNE
Aren't they good, though!
CONDUCTOR
Are you ready to go on?
NORMAN
Quite ready! What is it you want us to rehearse?
ANNE
I bet I know!
PAMELA
"Help! Help! She's collapsed!"—for the umpteenth time!
GLADYS
We must do that one with orchestra! I always go wrong—I can't *think* fast enough!
CONDUCTOR
Listen, everyone, please! There are two scenes I must rehearse before we go right through the opera. I want to do both ensembles from the second scene. First "O why do you weep?" with Rowan and the children, and then "Help! Help! She's collapsed!"
GLADYS
Oh, good! Do give us a nice big beat for that one!
ANNE
Shall we do it with movements?

NORMAN

Yes, of course! Positions for "*O why do you weep!*"

PAMELA

Places, children! Take your places!

ANNE

John, you are in the centre of us.

[*They take their positions for "O why do you weep?"\* GLADYS, NORMAN and MAX move to the side out of the way.*]

NORMAN [*to the conductor*]

Before you begin, do remind them about that *diminuendo* in the first verse.

CONDUCTOR

Yes, I was coming to that. Children!—*Children!* . . .

PAMELA

Pay attention, children!

CONDUCTOR

I want you to notice one thing especially about the first verse. When you sing your line together—"*Father and mother are far away*"—you begin *pianissimo*, get louder in the second bar, and then you have a *diminuendo* on the long note. Don't forget the *diminuendo*, or we shan't hear John on his entry. Try that sentence with piano once,—"*Father and mother* . . ." Give them their notes, Robert!

The PIANO plays the chord, and the children sing:

Children [*singing*]   "*Father and mother are far aw-ay!* . . ."

CONDUCTOR

*Diminuendo!*—Good!

Sam [*singing*]   "*How shall I laugh for joy?*"

CONDUCTOR

All right! Now we'll go from the beginning. John, you give us the cue—"nine next birthday."

\* (Vocal Score No. x)

[*JOHN gives the cue, and the Conductor leads the Children and the Orchestra in "O why do you weep?"*]

Sam [*speaking*]
"It's time I began work, they say. I'll be nine next birthday."
Children [*speaking*]
"Only nine!"

### Ensemble [*Number X.*]

"O why do you weep through the working day?
    O why do you weep at your task, poor boy?
Father and mother are far away,
    How shall I laugh for joy?
O where is the home where your life was gay?
    O where is the home that you loved, poor boy?
Home is a hundred miles away,
    How shall I laugh for joy?
O what is the voice that you must obey?
    O what is the voice that you fear, poor boy?
Master is angry again today,
    How shall I laugh for joy?"

CONDUCTOR
Well done! But remember—there is a *diminuendo* in the last verse, too! "*Master is angry again today!*"—*diminuendo* on 'today.' Don't forget that. Now let us cut on to Number Thirteen—"*Help! Help! She's collapsed!*" Number Thirteen, orchestra!

GLADYS
Mr. Harper!
CONDUCTOR
Yes?
GLADYS
Please may we go back a little and run into this? I'd like to take it from the last verse of my song—before Juliet faints.

CONDUCTOR
>   We're awfully short of time!

GLADYS
>   It won't take a moment—really it won't!

CONDUCTOR
>   Well, if we must, I suppose we must. Sorry, orchestra! Four—five—six bars before Number Thirteen. Are you ready on stage?

ANNE
>   John, you ought to be in the cupboard for this!

PAMELA
>   Oh yes, he should!

ANNE
>   Get in quickly.

>   [*JOHN scrambles into the toy cupboard.*]

>   Ready, Mr. Harper

CONDUCTOR
>   One bar before Miss Baggott's entry

>   [*The Orchestra plays and they sing:*]\*

MISS BAGGOTT
>   "Toys must be tidied up completely.
>   Come over here, you girls and boys.
>   Pack them away and stack them neatly.
>   Time that you tidied up your toys!
>   
>   [*MISS BAGGOTT stoops to open the cupboard.
>   JULIET screams and faints dramatically.*]

JULIET
>   Owwww . . . wwww!

## Ensemble [Number XIII.]

MISS BAGGOTT
>   Help! Help! She's collapsed!
>   A fit of the vapours!
>   She's fainted! Stand back!
>   Fetch feathers and tapers!

\* (Vocal Score No. XII)

ROWAN
>   Quick, lift up her head!
>   Rub her hands! Fetch some water!
>   We'll put her to bed
>   How lucky you caught her!

CHILDREN
>   Poor Juliet's ill!
>   Look how she's lying.
>   So silent and still
>   Can she be dying?
>   Her cheeks are so white,
>   Pale alabaster!
>   O dear! what a sight!
>   What a disaster!

CONDUCTOR
>   Everyone, you *must* watch my beat, or you'll be all over the place!

MONICA
>   Do we have to look straight at you?

CONDUCTOR
>   I don't mind where you look, so long as you see me.

RALPH
>   We need eyes in the back of our heads!

NORMAN [*from the side of the stage*]
>   Don't be silly, Ralph! I'm looking straight at you, but I can still see the conductor out of the corner of one eye.

RALPH
>   Can you? You must be double-jointed!

GLADYS
>   Have you finished with us, Mr. Harper.

CONDUCTOR
>   Yes, thank you!—Oh, no, I haven't! I want you to help me with the Coaching Song, please. Then you

can pull the curtain and get ready while I rehearse the other audience songs.

NORMAN

House lights again, Bruce!
[*BRUCE goes off stage to switch them on.*]
Coaching Song, everyone! Don't bother about position. Just sing it.

[*The HOUSE LIGHTS come up and the Conductor turns to rehearse the audience in their last song,\* the cast singing the verse each time.*]
At the end of this:

CONDUCTOR

Thank you, everyone on stage! I've finished with you for a few minutes. Close the curtain!

NORMAN

Hold on a moment! [*He comes centre stage and speaks to the audience.*] Ladies and gentlemen—and children! I just want to tell you from all of us on the stage that we are very sorry to have kept you waiting for the dress-rehearsal. You can see how much we have had to do—putting the scenery up, lighting, rehearsing and a hundred other little jobs. But honestly we are ready now—well, nearly ready! By the time Mr. Harper has rehearsed the other songs with you, we'll be champing to begin. Thank you for being so patient, goodbye for now — and we all hope you will like our little opera! Curtain! Pull the curtain!

EVERYONE [*waving and smiling*]
Goodbye! Goodbye for now!

[*The Curtain closes.
The Conductor turns to the audience and rehearses them in Sammy's Bath and the Night Song.† When this is done he announces a short*

---

\* (Vocal Score No. XVIII)  † (Vocal Score Nos. IX and XIV)

*interval, while he goes to make sure that everything is ready and to wish the singers 'Good Luck.' He asks the audience to be back ready for the Overture in ten minutes [or whatever length of interval is wanted.]*

THE END OF ACT TWO

# ACT THREE

## THE LITTLE SWEEP
A CHILDREN'S OPERA IN THREE SCENES

### SCENE ONE

*The scene is the nursery of Iken Hall, Suffolk, in January, 1810. The room is large and gaily-decorated and has two doors, a window and a large fireplace. There is a toy-cupboard at one side of the fireplace, an armchair and a rocking-horse. The room is swathed in dust-sheets at the beginning of Scene One, but these are cleared away before Scene Two.*

*AUDIENCE—FIRST SONG, to be sung before the curtain rises.*

1. Sweep! Sweep!
   Saddle your donkey and set on your way!
   There's chimneys need sweeping at Iken today
   Bring brushes and scrapers and baskets and sacks
   To harvest the soot from our chim-in-ey stacks.

2. Black Bob is coming and with him his lad,
   A sullen apprentice as black as his Dad,
   Their cries as they ride through the sharp morning air
   Set partridges drumming and startle the hare.

3.  Sam is the white boy, and sweep is his job,
    His father has sold him to cruel Black Bob.
    Today is his black day: today he must climb
    A chim-in-ey stack for the very first time.

4.  Snape lies behind them, and over the bridge
    They strike to the left by a narrowing ridge;
    Then follow the wandering dyke where it leads
    Through thickets of rushes and tussocks of reeds.

    [*The curtain rises, showing the nursery of Iken Hall. The Sweeps enter, singing.*]

1.  Sweep! Sweep!
    Saddle your donkey and set on your way!
    There's chimneys need sweeping at Iken today.
    Bring brushes and scrapers and baskets and sacks
    To harvest the soot from our chim-in-ey stacks.

    [*Miss Baggott, the housekeeper, follows the Sweeps into the room. She is elderly and sharp-tongued. Black Bob is the sweep-master, sullen and oafish, carrying a great coil of ropes.*
    *His son Clem carries an armful of brushes and sacks.*
    *Last of all comes Sam, looking miserable and tearstained, with three buckets on each arm and a coil of black rope slung across his chest. He looks very small and white beside the others. Rowan, the nursery-maid, who is laying dust-sheets over the furniture, is shocked by his wretchedness.*
    *During the following Trio, Miss Baggott gives impatient orders, Rowan watches the unhappy Sam, and the two Sweeps assemble their tools.*]

## Trio

MISS BAGGOTT
>Sweep this chimney, then next door!
>Hurry, Rowan! don't stand gaping!
>Four more chimneys on this floor.
>Give them all a thorough scraping!
>
>Filthy rascals, don't you dare
>Spread your soot around my attics!
>Lawks-a-mercy, I declare
>Sweeps are worse than the rheumatics!

ROWAN [of Sam]
>Small and white and stained with tears,
>Wrapped in scarecrow rags and patches,
>Faint with terror, full of tears,
>Wretched child whom sorrow catches.
>
>Torn from play and sold for pay,
>Taught a trade with kicks and curses,
>What can he do but obey—
>Meekly glad of little mercies?

BLACK BOB }
CLEM      }
>Chimbley-sweepers must 'ave boys,
>Same as poachers must 'ave ferrets.
>Brushes, rods and suchlike toys
>Can't compete with 'uman merits.
>
>Choose 'em nimble, spry and thin—
>That's the chap for chimbley-sweeping!
>Easy, too, for breaking in,
>Bar a bit of tears and weeping.

## Dialogue

MISS BAGGOT
>Hurry, Rowan! Sheets next door! [*She hurries off.*]

ROWAN
    Mister Sweep! for mercy's sake, don't send that little white boy up the chimney! He's weeping for fear!
BLACK BOB
    Fear—? Lor' bless you, them's tears of gratitude! He's aching for it, ain't you, Sam?
        [*Bob and Clem laugh horribly. Rowan runs from the room in distress. The Sweeps turn menacingly on Sam, pull off his clothes, tie a rope round his waist, and despite his struggles, drag him over to the hearth.*]

## Duet

BLACK BOB }
CLEM      }
    Now, little white boy!
    Shiver-with-fright boy!
    Scared-in-the-night boy!
        Time for your climb!

    Clothes off, my bright boy!
    Don't kick and fight, boy!
    Oh! so you'd bite, boy—?
        Time for your climb!

    Pull the rope tight, boy!
    Kiss us goodnight, boy!
    Climb out of sight, boy!
        Time for your climb!
            [*They have lifted poor Sam to the mouth of the chimney to catch the first climbing-rung. Bob hastens him with a terrifying shout.*]
BLACK BOB [*shouting*]
    Scrape that flue clean, or I'll roast you alive!
        [*Sam's legs hurriedly disappear up the flue.*]

65

When he comes back, boy!—
He'll be a black boy!
Scraper-and-sack boy!
Crawl-through-a-crack boy!
A chim-bley stack boy!
   Covered with grime!
[*The Sweeps collect their tools, and go out laughing.
The room is empty. Only the rope dangling in the hearth shows that the chimney is occupied. There is a distant sound of children's voices.*]

CHILDREN
   Juliet! we're coming!
   [*The door opens gently. Juliet slips in, shuts it carefully behind her and crosses to an armchair covered with a dust-sheet. Nearer cries from the children.*]
BOYS [*far*]
   Try the apple room—!
GIRLS [*far*]
   No! the linen cupboard—!
TWINS [*near*]
   Wait for us!
   [*Juliet slips into the chair beneath the sheet. The door flies suddenly open and the Twins pop their heads in.*]
TWINS
   She's not in here!
GAY [*far*]
   Hughie—!
SOPHIE [*far*]
   Tina—!
TWINS
   Wait for US—!
   [*They disappear hurriedly. Juliet pokes her head above the sheet, emerges and approaches the door. It begins slowly to open. She scurries back to*

>            *her hiding-place as Johnnie peeps in. He makes*
>            *for her chair.*]

CHILDREN [*far*]
    Harness-room—!
>            [*Johnnie pulls the sheet from the chair, revealing*
>            *Juliet.*]

JOHNNIE
    Caught you!
JULIET
    Quick, Johnnie! You hide, too!
    There's lots of room for me and you!
>            [*They both hide in the chair with the sheet over*
>            *them.*]

CHILDREN [*far*]
    Johnnie! Johnnie! Where ARE you—?
>            [*Giggles from underneath the sheet. Suddenly the*
>            *rope in the fireplace begins to waggle violently,*
>            *and Sam shouts.*]

SAM [*from the chimney*]
    Help! Help! I'm stuck!
JULIET }
JOHNNIE } [*showing themselves*]
    What's that?
SAM [*from the chimney*]
    Help! Pull me down!
JULIET
    It's a sweep-boy!
JOHNNIE
    In the flue!
CHILDREN [*near*]
    Johnnie! Johnnie! Where are *you?*
SAM [*from the chimney*]
    Help! Help!
JULIET
    Call the others quickly, John!

CHILDREN [*bursting into the nursery*]
   Here we are! What's going on?
JULIET }
JOHNNIE }
   Ssssh!
SAM [*from the chimney*]
   Help! I'm suffocating!
JULIET
   Pull him down!
JOHNNIE
   It's no good waiting!
      [*All the children move to the fireplace. Juliet calls up the chimney.*]
JULIET
   Hold very tight, and don't let go!
   We'll pull the rope from down below!
      [*The Children pick up the rope, ready to pull.*]
BOYS
   Ready?
SAM [*from the chimney*]
   Ready!

## Shanty

ALL CHILDREN
   Pull the rope gently until he is free!
      Pull O! Heave O!
   Pull the rope gently until he is free!
      Pull O! Heave O!
SAM [*from the chimney*]
   No good!
JULIET
   Pull harder this time—but not *too* hard!

ALL
>   Pull the rope harder and give a good heave!
>         Pull O! Strongly O!
>   Pull the rope harder and give a good heave!
>         Pull O! Strongly O!

SAM [*tearfully*]
>   I'm still stuck!

ALL
>   Pull the rope smartly with one two three jerk!
>         One two, three, Jerk!
>   Pull the rope smartly with one two three jerk!
>         One, two, three, JERK—

SAM
>   OWWWWWWWWWW!!!!!!!!!
>   [*With a loud scream, Sam descends in an avalanche of soot and stones, and lies flat in the hearth.*]

CHILDREN [*scared*]
>   Oooooohhhh—!!!!

TWINS }
SOPHIE }
>   You've killed him!
>   [*the children anxiously surround Sam and lift him, bringing out their handkerchiefs to wipe his tears. He is desperate with grief and fear.*]

## Ensemble

CHILDREN
>   Is he wounded? Please forgive us!
>       Are you very much in pain?
>       All we wanted was to help you.

SAM
>   *Please* don't send me up again!

CHILDREN
>Poor young boy! He's just a baby!
>Weak with toil and wan with strain.
>Fancy making him sweep chimneys!

SAM    *Please* don't send me up again!

CHILDREN
>Will Miss Baggot let us keep him?
>No, she won't! We'd ask in vain.
>She'd betray him to his master.

SAM    *Please* don't send me up again!

CHILDREN
>Can't we rescue him from sweeping?
>Hide him safe? And not explain
>Till the sweeps have gone and left him?

SAM    *Please* don't send me up again!

CHILDREN
>*We* won't send you up again!


*Recitative*

GAY
>Hide him *here*, among our toys!

JOHNNIE
>Room enough for twenty boys!

OTHERS
>Quickly, then!

JULIET
>But wait! I say!—
>*They* must think he's run away!

SOPHIE
>Through the window!

TWINS
>Down the creeper!

BOYS
> Come one, little chimney-sweeper!
> [*The children escort Sam across the room, planting his feet to make tracks on the sheets, while Hughie and Tina stretch the rope with its empty noose pointing towards the window.*]

## Marching Song

CHILDREN
> Sooty tracks upon the sheet,
> Sooty marks of sooty feet,
> Soot upon the window-seat
>     Make our evidence complete!
>
> Soot upon the window-sill,
> Soot applied with loving skill,
> Soot to blind their eyes, until
>     Down they gulp our sooty pill!
>
> Clamber up and smudge the brick!
> Just a little—not too thick!
> There's our disappearing trick . . .!
>     Someone's coming!
>         Hide him!
>             QUICK! . . .
>
> [*The children carry Sam swiftly to the toy-cupboard, bundle him inside, snatch up his ragged clothes, and dive under the shrouded furniture, just as Miss Baggott enters, followed by Bob and Clem, with Rowan behind them.*]

## Dialogue

MISS BAGGOTT
> Half-past eleven! Hurry, you idlers! Attics next!

BLACK BOB
    Yaps just like a little old fox-terrier!
CLEM
    Real old blunderbuss, ain't she!
MISS BAGGOTT
    What's this—? Window open—!
        [*They observe the signs of Sam's disappearance.*]

*Marching Song—Repeated as Trio*

    Sooty-tracks—upon the—sheet . . .
    Soot—upon the—window-seat . . .
    Sooty-rope and—Sooty-noose . . .
      After him! Young Sammy's loose . . .!
        [*Bob runs to the hearth and gives a blood-curdling yell.*]
BOB
    S — A — M————————!!!
                [*There is no answer.*]
CLEM
    S — A — M————————!!!

*Trio—Furioso*

    Wait until we catch him; we'll whip him till he howls!
    We'll teach him to run off and leave his duty!
    Chain him up and kennel him; keep him with the fowls!
    And mortify his pride, the little beauty!
        [*The Sweeps turn and run off, shouting furiously. Miss Baggott follows, calling them back.*]
BLACK BOB
    I'll give him *Run Away!* I'll keel-haul 'im round Snape Bridge!

CLEM
    Lily-livered toad! Tar an' feather him!
MISS BAGGOTT
    Come back, you blackguards! Six more chimneys!
    Come back . . .!
        [*The Sweeps and Miss Baggott have gone. Rowan, thinking herself alone, gives way to her distress for Sammy.*]

*Song—Rowan*

Run, poor sweepboy! Run much faster!
    Run with all your might and main!
Close behind you comes your master,
    Mad to bring you back again.

Far along the frozen river,
    Sharp across the frosty air,
Distant echoes make Sam shiver,
    Fill his heart with new despair.

Run, poor boy! O do not slacken!
    Black Bob follows swift behind!
See his angry features blacken!
    Rage and fury make him blind.

How I wish that I could save you!
    I would hide you far away
From those tyrants who enslave you
    And torment you day by day!

    [*During the last verse of this song the children's heads emerge from under their coverings, unnoticed by Rowan. They watch her in admiration. She gives a gasp of surprise when she realises that they are watching. They stand up and beam at her.*]

## Recitative

JOHNNIE
   Dear Rowan . . .!
SOPHIE
   Dear, dear Rowan . . .!
JULIET
   Dearest Rowan . . .!
GAY
   Dearest, darling Rowan . . .!
TWINS
   Dear, dearest, darlingest Rowan . . .!
ROWAN
   What does this mean?
CHILDREN [Mysteriously]
   Ssssssh!!

   [They open the cupboard door and beckon. Sam pokes out a timid and very sooty head.]

## Dialogue

ROWAN
   Goodness gracious me! The Little Sweep!
CHILDREN
   OUR Little Sweep!
ROWAN
   But whatever will Miss Baggot say to him?
GAY
   She doesn't know . . .
JOHNNIE
   She needn't know . . .
JULIET
   And she's *not* to know!
TWINS
   He's a Secret!

ROWAN
    But what are you going to do with him?
TWINS
    Feed him . . .!
SOPHIE
    The poor boy's hungry.
JULIET
    You see, Rowan, we can't possibly hand him over to those horrible sweeps, can we . . .?
        [Rowan hesitates, so the children answer for her.]
CHILDREN
    No—!
JULIET
    . . . we can't possibly tell mama, 'cos she's away . . .
GAY
    Seeing papa off! to join his ship!
JULIET
    . . . we can't possibly tell Miss Baggott . . .
TWINS
    'Cos she'd turn him out of the house!
JULIET
    . . . so you are the only grown-up we can tell!
ROWAN
    That's all very well for you, Miss Juliet, and for Master Gay and Miss Sophie, I daresay, but you must remember that your cousins and I are only visitors in your house . . .
JULIET [interrupting]
    Never mind about cousins and visitors! This is our latest visitor, and when you have a visitor who is cold and hungry and covered with soot from top to toe, what do you do with him . . .?
TWINS
    BATH him—!
GAY
    Of course you do!

SOPHIE
> But what about Miss Baggott?

JOHNNIE
> Oh, bother Miss Baggott!

ROWAN
> You need not worry for a little. I saw her crossing the courtyard in her clogs.

JOHNNIE
> Hooray! She's following the sweeps!

GAY
> That gives us an hour to play with . . .

ROWAN
> I'm sure I don't know if you are doing right, Miss Juliet . . .

JULIET [*firmly*]
> Look at him!—*Does* he need a bath, or doesn't he?

CHILDREN
> *Yes!*

ROWAN
> Would you like to have a bath, Sammy?

SAM
> Yes, please, Miss!

JULIET
> Then you go and fill the buckets, Rowan . . .

ROWAN
> There's warm water on the hob . . .

TWINS
> We'll fetch the bath from the attic . . .!

SOPHIE
> I'll get some clothes from Johnnie's box . . .!

JOHNNIE
> I'll carry water . . .!

GAY
> I'll light the fire . . .!

JULIET
> I'll fetch soap and towels . . .! Is that all clear?

ALL
> Yes!

JULIET
> Then you stay in your cupboard, Sammy, and in five minutes we'll all be back for the Grand Transformation Scene!

ALL
> Come on—!

[*The children scatter eagerly as the curtain falls.*]

END OF SCENE ONE

*Interlud*

*Audience—Song Tv*

[*The Conductor invites the audience to sing the Song of Sam's Bath.*]

1. The kettles are singing
   Like midsummer larks,
   The fire is flinging
   A shower of sparks:
   The children run flying
   To fetch what they're bidden,
   For washing and drying
   The sweep-boy they've hidden.

2. They hurry upstairs to
   The nursery hearth,
   Where Rowan prepares to
   Give Sammy his bath:
   With brushes to scrub him,
   With basins to flood him,
   With flannels to rub him,
   With soap-balls to sud him.

3. *Spa-lash!* in he plunges,
  And Rowan lets fly
 With sopping-wet sponges
  And sparks in her eye!
 She washes and rinses
  And scrubbs willy-nilly,
 Till poor Sammy winces
  But shines like a lily!

4. And now Sam is gleaming
  Like snow in the sun,
 While Rowan stands beaming
  To see her work done.
 So all who were frightened
  When Sam was benighted,
 Please see how he's whitened
  And show you're delighted!

## SCENE TWO

[*The Curtain rises. All the children are watching the new Sam as he stands clutching a towel and grinning. Rowan is on her knees beside him. The children sing the following continuation of the Audience's song, while Sam finishes drying.*]

CHILDREN and ROWAN
5. O Sammy is whiter
  Than swans as they fly,
 O Sammy is brighter
  Than stars in the sky!

6.        O Sam is as fair as
            The white-foaming seas,
          Or spindrift in air, as
            Waves challenge the breeze.
          The hateful employment
            He suffered so blindly
          Gives way to enjoyment . . .
SAM
            And THANK you all kindly!

*Spoken Dialogue*

ROWAN
   Quick, children! We must tidy the room before Miss Baggot comes back.
JULIET
   Just one moment, Rowan! Tell me, Sammy, haven't you any father or mother?
SAM
   Yes, Miss.
GAY
   Then where are they?
SAM
   At home . . .
JOHNNIE
   Where's home?
SAM
   Little Glemham.
ROWAN
   Little Glemham?—But I come from near Glemham myself! Whose boy are you?
SAM
   Dad's name is Sparrow the waggoner.
ROWAN
   Josiah Sparrow, from along the ten-acre field?
SAM
   That's him, Miss.

JULIET
    And he sold you to that wicked sweep . . .?
JOHNNIE
    Sold you . . .?
SOPHIE
    For money . . .?
GAY
    Sold his own son . . .?
TWINS
    How *could* he . . .!
SAM
    He didn't want to, but he broke his hip last threshing-time, and there wasn't anything to eat . . .
ROWAN
    Poor man!
CHILDREN
    Poor Sammy!
SAM
    But it's time I began work, they say. I shall be nine next birthday.
CHILDREN [shocked]
    Only nine . . .!

    [*The children are dismayed and unhappy to hear what Sammy has told them. They turn sadly to their task of tidying the room and help Sam into the clean clothes they have found for him.*]

*Song*

CHILDREN, ROWAN and SAM
    O why do you weep
        Through the working day?
    O why do you weep
        At your task, poor boy?
           Father and mother are far away.
           How shall I laugh and play?

O where is the home
   Where your life was gay?
O where is the home
   That you loved, poor boy?
      Home is a hundred miles away.
      How shall I laugh and play?

O what is that voice
   That you must obey?
O what is that voice
   That you fear, poor boy?
      Master is angry again today.
      How shall I laugh and play?

## Dialogue

JOHNNIE
   I have an idea!
JULIET
   What is it?
JOHNNIE
   Rowan! when will you be packing our trunks?
ROWAN
   Tonight, when you are in bed.
JOHNNIE
   Will you leave an empty space in the top of mine?
GAY
   I see! Put Sammy in the trunk . . .
JULIET
   And take him home with you!
SOPHIE
   Oh, yes!
TWINS
   Hooray!
ROWAN
   But he'll stifle in a trunk . . .!

GAY
  No, he won't.
JULIET
  You can let him out as soon as you are clear of the house.
ROWAN
  I can't think what your father and mother will say to him.
JOHNNIE
  They'll help us, I'm positive they will!
ROWAN
  And where will you keep him for tonight?
GAY
  In the cupboard! It's the only place.
TWINS [*at the windows*]
  Quick! Quick! She's coming!
JULIET
  Who's coming?
TWINS
  Miss Baggott!
GAY
  Where?
SOPHIE
  Through the garden gate!
ALL
  Hurry! Hide Sammy! Tidy the room!

*Hurry Music*

[*Sam leaps into the toy-cupboard, Gay and Johnnie carry the hip bath out, Sophie takes the towel horse, Rowan and Juliet whisk off the remaining dust-sheets.*
*Then the children make a sedate tableau around the fire. The boys are reading, Rowan winds wool from a skein held by Juliet, the Twins are busy with a quiet game.*

[*Miss Baggott comes up to the nursery in hat and boots, irritated, angry and tired, and eager to vent her indignation.*]


*Recitative and Aria*

MISS BAGGOTT.
Ah! . . . Blackguards! Blackamoors! Brutes! . . . Oh! my poor feet! . . . [*she sits.*] The vermin! All the way to Snape and back! . . . Oh, my joints! . . . Never, never—in all my born days! . . . "Come back!" says I, "Come back and finish your lawful work" Their language! The insults! Drat the sweeps,—for they that mock shall be a nay-word and a by-word, and the good shall trample them underfoot! . . . Accused me, ME!, of hiding their beastly boy! I'll hide him, if once I lay my hands on him!
    [*Suspicious of the silence, she casts an eagle eye around her.*]
Curtain's crooked, Rowan! Carelessness! Slapdashery! Help me up!
    [*The children assist her to rise heavily from the chair. She moves slowly round the room and inspects it.*]

    Look at the creases in that curtain!
    Look at the footprints on the floor!
    *You* haven't tidied up, that's certain.
    Look at that filthy cupboard-door!

    Fireplace is grubby, fender *covered!*
    Bother Black Bob and both his boys!
    Smudges of soot all round the cupboard!
    Have you arranged the children's toys?

Toys must be tidied up completely.
Come over here, you girls and boys!
Open the door and pack them neatly.
Time that you tidied up your toys.

[*Miss Baggott moves determinedly towards the toy-cupboard, and her hand is out-stretched to grasp the handle and open the door.*
*The children are on tip-toe with alarm, when suddenly a loud and penetrating sigh, like a pricked balloon, distracts her. She turns to see Juliet collapse full-length on the floor.*
*All is confusion as they surround the prostrate girl.*]

JULIET [*fainting*]
 Aaaah————hhh!

*Ensemble*

MISS BAGGOTT
 Help! Help! She's collapsed!
 A fit of the vapours!
 She's fainted! Stand back!
 Fetch feathers and tapers!

ROWAN
 Quick! Lift up her head!
 Rub her hands! Bring some water!
 We'll put her to bed!
 How lucky you caught her!

CHILDREN
 Poor Juliet's ill!
 Look how she's lying!
 So silent and still—
 Can she be dying?

Her cheeks are so white—
Pale alabaster!
Oh dear, what a sight!
What a disaster!
   [*Juliet is lifted and carried into the next room by Rowan and Miss Baggott, while the children frisk around in a frenzy of excitement and relief.*]

CHILDREN
   Blankets! Feathers! Warming-pan!
   Run as quickly as you can!
   Brandy! Sal volatile!
   Barley water! Cups of tea!
   Lift her legs!—no, keep her flat!
   Any simpleton knows that.
   Raise her head! Undo her frock!
   Cold for fever! Warmth for shock!
      [*As Juliet disappears through the door among a crowd of over-zealous helpers, Johnnie opens the cupboard door, and calls out—*]

JOHNNIE
   Sit tight, Sammy! Tomorrow you're a free man!
      [*The children dance with triumph at the way Juliet has saved them.*]

CHILDREN
   Juliet has won the day
   In a very simple way!
   Sam is safe—and he can stay
   In his hiding place—Hooray!

[*The* CURTAIN *closes on them.*]

THE END OF SCENE TWO

## Interlude

[*The Conductor invites the Audience to sing the Night Song.*]

AUDIENCE

The owl, wide-winging through the sky
In search of mice and lesser fry,
Repeats his loud, unhappy cry—
              Tu-whoo! Tu-whoo!

The heron listens, gaunt and still,
Within his nest upon the hill,
Then parts a stern and savage bill—
              Kaaah! Kaaah!

The turtle dove begins to stir,
Removes the leaves that shelter her,
And answers with melodious purr
              Prroo! Prroo!

The chaffinch and his mate rejoice
To exercise their singing voice.
They take the descant for their choice—
              Pink! Pink! Pink!

From North and South and East and West
The birds compete for who sings best,
But who shall choose the loveliest?

[*Loudly*] {
  TU-WHOO! TU-WHOO!
  KAAAH! KAAAH!
  PROO! PROO!
  PINK! PINK! PINK!
}

The night is past, the owl is hoarse,
The finches slumber in the gorse,
The heron stoops, the turtle droops,—

[*Softly*] {
  TU-WHOO ! TU-WHOO !
  KAAAH ! KAAAH !
  PRROO ! PRROO !
  PINK ! PINK ! PINK !
}

## SCENE THREE

[*The following morning. Rowan has just entered the nursery with a breakfast-tray for Juliet, who is wearing a warm quilted dressing-gown. She puts the tray down and they go to the cupboard to fetch Sammy.*]

### Dialogue

ROWAN
  Breakfast, Sammy!
JULIET
  Ham and eggs!
ROWAN
  Stretch yourself—
JULIET
  And kick your legs!
ROWAN
  Only twenty minutes more
  Till the coach is at the door!
    [*Rowan hurries off again. Sam stretches himself.*]
JULIET
  Hungry, Sammy?
SAMMY
  Oh yes, Miss!
JULIET
  Eat away then, while I unstrap this trunk.
    [*Sam sits at the table and begins to eat. Juliet unstraps the trunk, singing.*]

### Song

JULIET
  Soon the coach will carry you away
    And we shall wave Goodbye! and laugh to see
  The little sweep we rescued yesterday
    Set off along the road to liberty.

Black you were, you poor unhappy mite,
And very ugly too, I must confess!
Today you're guinea-bright and gleaming white,
And radiant with joy and happiness.

Sammy dear, today at last you're free!
Your cruel apprenticeship is at an end.
Accept this gift from Sophie, Gay and me
To show our fondness for our new young friend.

[*Juliet holds out to Sammy three shining half-crowns.*]

## Dialogue

SAMMY
Oh no, Miss! I couldn't accept it, really I couldn't, though it's very kindly meant . . .
JULIET
Please do take it, Sammy!
SAMMY
But I've never seen so much money in my life!
JULIET
Then put it in your pocket and you'll be a rich man!
SAMMY
Oh, but, Miss . . . !
JULIET
Quickly! Here come the others!
[*Juliet goes to the door, and Sam stands ready to hide if need be. The other children rush in, one by one, followed by Rowan.*]

## Ensemble—Children and Sam

JOHNNIE
'Morning, Sammy! Lovely weather
For our journey home together!

SOPHIE
    'Morning, Sammy! You look splendid
    Now your sweeping-days are ended!
GAY
    'Morning, Sammy! Time to travel!
    I hear coachwheels on the gravel!
TWINS
    'Morning, Sammy! We're delighted
    That you're safe!—and so excited!
ALL
    'Morning, Sammy! 'Morning! 'Morning!

## Dialogue

JOHNNIE
    The coach is coming—
GAY
    Into the trunk with you!
ROWAN
    I'll fetch your hats and coats and mufflers.
                                          [*She goes off to get them.*]
JULIET
    In you jump!
GAY
    Take some bread and butter with you.
                                           [*Sam gets into the trunk.*]
JULIET
    Goodbye, Sammy dear, and very good luck!
                                                           [*She kisses him.*]
SOPHIE
    Goodbye, dear Sammy!                [*She kisses him.*]
GAY
    Jolly good luck to you, Sammy!       [*Handshake.*]
JOHNNIE
    Goodbye for now, Sammy!
TWINS
    Goodbye! Goodbye!

ROWAN [*returning with hats and coats*]
   Hurry, children! The coach is at the door! Goodbye for now, Sammy, dear!
       [*Juliet and Gay hastily strap up the trunk, while Sophie watches at the door, and Rowan helps Johnnie and the Twins into their travelling clothes.*]
SOPHIE
   Quickly! Quickly! Quickly! I can hear voices!
GAY
   Finished!
JULIET [*kneeling by the trunk*]
   Are you all right, Sammy?
SAM [*muffled from inside*]
   Yes, thank you, Miss! Very comfortable.
       [*The children clap their hands in silent glee.*]
MISS BAGGOTT [*off*]
   Come along, the pair of you! Mind the paint, or I'll know the reason why!
       [*She enters the room followed by Tom, the coachman from Woodbridge, who is muffled up in an enormous overcoat, and by Alfred, the gardener, in apron and leggings. They are not a bit afraid of Miss Baggott.*]
TOM
   Whoo! Stairs took me wind away! Whoo!
ALFRED
   Terrible old house for stairs, this.
MISS BAGGOTT
   That's the trunk and mind the corners!
TOM
   Whoa, Missus, whoa! Mustn't flog a willing horse! Easy does it!
ALFRED
   Them stairs catch me a slap in my lumbago.

*MISS BAGGOTT*
  Come along, my men!
*TOM*
  Gently, Ma, gently with the bearing rein!—How's that strong right arm of yours, Alfred lad?
*ALFRED*
  It's the small of the back does me, Tom. The spirit's willing, but the small of the back says "Careful, Alfred, careful!"
*TOM*
  Shall we take a dab at that little old trunk?
*ALFRED*
  No hurry, Tom. Whenever you're certain of your breath and suchlike.
*TOM*
  Now, let's understand each other, Alfred boy. When I says *three* we lift, if you take my meaning. 'One—Two—Three,' and up she'll come like the morning lark.
  [*The two men bend down together and take a grip of the handles, but find the trunk too heavy to lift.*]

## TRIO—TOM, ALFRED AND MISS BAGGOTT

*TOM*  
*ALFRED* }
  Ready, Alfred? Up she goes!
  Gently does it. Mind your toes.
  One and two and—Wait for me!
  Sorry, Alfred! One, two, three—?
  One and two and *three* and lift!
  No, the dratted thing won't shift!
  What's inside it? Full of books!
  Twice as heavy as it looks.

Come along, we'll carry it below.
Feels like screwed down to the floor.

Full of stones or sand or such.
Weighs like lead, but twice as much.

MISS BAGGOTT
Heave it up and off you go!
Hurry, carry it below!

What a stupid fuss to make
About a trunk, for goodness' sake!

Can't you lift one little box
Packed with shoes and shirts and socks?

*Recitative*

TOM
Can't be done, Missus!
ALFRED
Much too heavy!
MISS BAGGOTT
Nonsense! I packed it myself.
TOM
Then you'll have to unpack it.
MISS BAGGOTT
I'll do nothing of the sort.
TOM
Then here she stays!
MISS BAGGOTT
The impertinence!
TOM
Either that there box is unpacked . . .
ALFRED
. . . or we leave her where she lies!
CHILDREN
Oh, *no!*

ALFRED }
TOM    }
    Oh, yes!
ROWAN
    Mister Tom, we'll help you lift the box!
CHILDREN
    Yes, please let us help!
TOM
    Well, that's a fair offer, Miss, and kindly meant.
    What's your view, Alfred?
ALFRED
    Very kind indeed!
ROWAN
    Good!—everyone help lift!
        [*All, except Miss Baggott, gather round the trunk.*]

## Ensemble

ALL
    One and Two and—That's the way!
    Up she comes! Hip-hip-hooray!
    Willing hands make labour light.
    Now you'll manage her alright!
        [*The men go off with the trunk. Miss Baggott follows them, calling "Mind the paint! Don't drop it! Easy round the corners!" The children heave a deep sigh of relief.*]

## Dialogue

CHILDREN and ROWAN
    He's gone, thank goodness, on his way!
    —And thank you for our holiday!
    Goodbye, my dears, goodbye!
        [*In great haste Rowan, Johnnie and the Twins hurry off, leaving Gay, Juliet and Sophie alone.*]

GAY
   Quick! Open the window!
JULIET
   Look! There's the trunk! They're lifting it into the coach!
SOPHIE
   He's safe at last! Sammy's safe!
GAY
   There come the others! They're climbing into the coach!
JULIET  ⎫
GAY     ⎬ [*calling*]
SOPHIE  ⎭
   Goodbye, Rowan! Goodbye, Johnnie! Goodbye, Twins!
VOICES [*off*]
   Goodbye! Goodbye!
JULIET  ⎫
GAY     ⎬ [*very quietly*]
SOPHIE  ⎭
   And goodbye, Sammy!—dear Sammy!
GAY
   Tom's on his box . . .!
JULIET
   He's lifting his whip . . .!
ALL
   And away they go!
   [*The whole cast has come quickly back on stage. They improvise a coach with the trunk, the rocking-horse and a chair or two. The Twins kneel in front twirling parasols for wheels, Sam rides proudly on the horse, Tom the coachman flourishes his whip, and all sway in time with the song as they travel away down the high road.*]

## Coaching Song

The horses are champing, eagerly stamping,
   *Crack!* goes the whip, as the coachman lets slip!
      So there! So there! Good brown mare,
      Lead away at a spanking trot.

The gravel is churning. Look! they are turning
   Off to the right, and away from our sight.
      So there! So there! Good brown mare,
      Lead away at a spanking trot.

They swing from the bye-road on to the high-road,
   Gathering pace for the home-again race!
      Ho there! Let me see you canter!
      Canter, canter, good brown mare!

Now Sam has arisen out of his prison,
   Grinning with glee to be happy and free!
      Ho there! Let me see you canter!
      Canter, canter, good brown mare!

Our story is ended. You who've attended
   Join in the song as the coach runs along!
      Go there! Let me see you gallop!
      Gallop, gallop, good brown mare!

      Steady now, and slacken pace!
      Easy there! You've won the race!

   Time to stop—our journey's done.
   Goodbye to you everyone!

THE CURTAIN FAL

# NOTE ABOUT THE AUDIENCE SONGS

Most audiences are eager to sing once their initial shyness has been overcome. Experience shows that an average audience can learn these songs in about twenty minutes during the rehearsal that is allowed for in Act Two. They must of course have copies to sing from,* and it is an advantage if some of them have learnt the melodies beforehand.

It is suggested that the conductor should approach the audience-rehearsal in a friendly and informal manner, and should explain the special difficulties of each song before he begins to rehearse it. He will, for example, show them how to count four-five time in the first song and let them try singing "Sweep! . . . four-five! Sweep! . . . four-five!" once or twice. After hearing the melody played by the piano once, they will be able to sing it with piano accompaniment and then to sing it with orchestra.

For school-performances it would be a good thing to let the whole audience of children learn the songs in advance, so that they would be ready to perform them after a brief run-through in Act Two.

---

* The four audience-songs are published by Messrs. Boosey & Hawkes, Ltd.

www.ingramcontent.com/pod-product-compliance
Lightning Source LLC
Chambersburg PA
CBHW031255230426
43670CB00005B/198